ZOO BABIES

Sydney
the Koala

Story by **Georgeanne Irvine**
Photographs by **Ron Garrison**

of the **Zoological Society of San Diego**

School & Library Edition
CHILDRENS PRESS, CHICAGO

Library of Congress Cataloging in Publication Data

Irvine, Georgeanne.
  Sydney the koala.

  (Zoo babies)
  Includes index.
  Summary: A baby koala describes his growing
awareness of his zoo world after he becomes
too big for his mother's pouch.
    1. Koalas — Juvenile literature. 2. Animals,
Infancy of — Juvenile literature. 3. Zoo
animals — Juvenile literature. [1. Koalas.
2. Animals — Infancy. 3. Zoo animals]
I. Garrison, Ron, ill. II. Title.
III. Series.
QL737.M39I78   1982   599.2   82-9452
ISBN 0-516-09304-5   AACR2

ZOO BABIES

Sydney
the Koala

I'm Sydney, a baby koala at the Zoo. Being a baby koala can be a bit confusing at times.

Just after I was born, I lived in a warm and cozy place that was very dark. I felt so comfortable that all I wanted to do was sleep and eat.

As the months went by, my warm and cozy place seemed to be getting smaller! Maybe I was growing bigger! When I was six months old, I had a big surprise.

One day I stretched too much, and all of a sudden, things weren't dark anymore. I was surrounded by bright light—but I was sitting next to something warm and furry ...

my mama, Matilda!

Mama told me that after I was born, I crawled into her pouch to grow for awhile. No wonder it was so dark and cozy!

At first, I was only about the size of a bumblebee. I kept growing and growing until finally I grew too big and popped out of the pouch.

Coming out of a pouch for the first time can be scary. I felt much safer in Mama's pouch, but she told me not to worry.

I learned from Mama that only
certain animals called marsupials
ever get to live in pouches. Some
other marsupials besides koalas are

wombats,

kangaroos,

and wallabies.

Like me, these marsupials come from Australia.

Mama decided to take me exploring. She let me ride piggyback, so I wouldn't get lost or into mischief. We started moving along the tree branches very slowly. Koalas move slowly most of the time, but I hung on tightly anyway. I didn't want to fall to the ground!

The leaves smelled good. They were eucalyptus leaves. A leaf got into my mouth as we brushed past. It tasted so good, I ate it. Mama was happy that I liked it. Eucalyptus leaves are koala food. In fact, they are the only thing we eat!

Chomping on eucalyptus leaves
was fun for awhile, but I wanted to do
more! I thought it might be fun to
meet some other koalas. I was looking
at another koala called Gumdrop.
Then I saw something pick him up
that didn't look like a koala at all! It
was much bigger than a koala, and it
didn't have fur.

The thing turned out to be Jane, the koala keeper. She takes care of all of us koalas. One of her many jobs is making sure we get enough food.

Gumdrop was happy because Jane had just given him fresh eucalyptus leaves. He yawned and was ready for a nap. He snuggled up to a tree and was asleep in a few minutes.

Why would a koala want to take a nap when there's so much to explore? I wasn't frightened anymore. I wanted to say hello to the other koalas—but they were all falling asleep!

I discovered that koalas sleep a lot.

Soon I was sound asleep, too!

Facts About Koalas

Where found: Koalas are native only to Australia. They were once in danger of becoming extinct but are now protected by law.

Family: They are members of the group of marsupial animals, many of which are found only in Australia. All marsupial babies are very small and undeveloped when born. They live in pouches on the underside of their mothers' bodies until they have fur, until their eyes are open, and until they can cling to their mothers' backs.

Baby koalas: When born, koala cubs are only one inch or less long and about half as thick as a man's little finger. Only one baby is born at a time. It lives in its mother's pouch for about half a year. Then it begins to ride on its mother's back, but uses the pouch for sleeping for a few months. A baby koala needs to be taken care of by its mother for about four years until it is almost full grown.

Adult koalas: The fur of adult koalas is a gray brown color. They are from two to three feet high and weigh from twenty to thirty pounds. Their ears are big and furry. Their noses are black and shiny and look as if they were made of leather. Koalas have no tails. Each of their paws has five claws to help them climb trees.

Food: Koalas eat only one thing—the leaves of eucalyptus trees. Eucalyptus originally grew only in Australia and Asia. Now some are grown in the western part of the United States.

Sleeping: Koalas are nocturnal animals. That means they sleep during the day and move around at night, climbing trees and eating leaves.

Teddy bears: Many children's teddy bears look like koalas, although the koala is not really a bear. In fact, the first toy teddy bear, made in the early 1900s, was supposed to look like a grizzly bear, not a koala!

INDEX